PIGEONS

BY MIRIAM SCHLEIN

PHOTOGRAPHS BY

MARGARET MILLER

THOMAS Y. CROWELL

NEW YORK

Pigeons

Text copyright © 1989 by Miriam Schlein
Illustrations copyright © 1989 by Margaret Miller

Library of Congress Cataloging-in-Publication Data
Schlein, Miriam.
    Pigeons.

    Summary: Explains how pigeons—descendants of wild rock doves—live their lives, raise their young, and have been useful throughout history to people.
    1. Pigeons. [1. Pigeons] I. Miller, Margaret, 1945– ill. II. Title.
QL 696.C63S35   1989   598′.65   88-35286
ISBN 0-690-04808-4
ISBN 0-690-04810-6 (lib. bdg.)

Typography by Christine Kettner
1   2   3   4   5   6   7   8   9   10
First Edition

PIGEONS

In the city, there are pigeons all around. They march in little bunches along the sidewalk. They sit in rows on rooftops. They love to sit on statues.

Wherever you look, there they are. You can hear them, too.

Coo-roo...coo-roo.

Why do pigeons live in the city? You would think that birds would want to live where there are more trees.

City pigeons are descendants of wild rock doves, birds that nest high on cliffs and rock ledges.

Look around. Tall city buildings are like man-made "cliffs." And there are all kinds of ledges where pigeons can perch. Windowsills. Bridge beams. Steeples, towers, roofs. The pigeons feel at home. To them, the city is a natural place to live.

Because there are so many pigeons around, we take them for granted. We don't pay much attention to them. But watch them. You can see pigeons do some interesting things.

7

Close-up of a city pigeon

A city pigeon is about 11 inches long and weighs about 10 ounces. Most are gray, with a ring of glossy green and purple feathers around the neck. Some are black. A few are light brown, or creamy white with brown specks. Sometimes you see an all-white one.

Their heads bob back and
forth as they walk. Their little
round eyes are red or yellow,
and shine like glassy beads.

9

See the small white lump at the base of the bill? This is called the *cere*. It's tough flesh, like a callus. It protects the nose slits.

Pigeon toes are long, red, and skinny. Curled around, they get a firm grip on any edge.

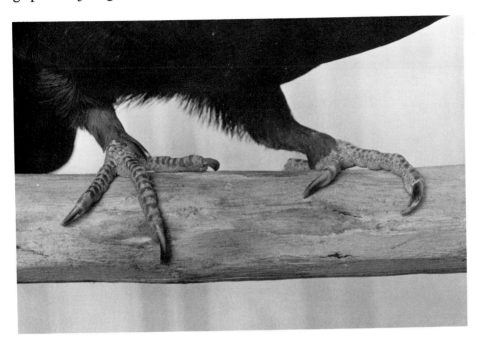

Sometimes you see what looks like a one-legged pigeon. But it may not be. The pigeon could be just standing on one foot. The other leg is pulled up to rest and is hidden in the feathers.

11

You might see pigeons taking a bath in a puddle. They flap their wings and ruffle their feathers so the water seeps in. When they get out, they flap some more to shed water, then sit in the sun to dry off.

In a snowstorm, if they have no shelter, they just brave it out. They sit on a ledge, hunched over, facing inward, and wait for the storm to end.

You might see a pigeon standing on the ground flapping its wings but not taking off. What's it doing? It's exercising, to keep its wing muscles in shape.

The wings are pointy; the tail is straight-edged. In flight, it spreads out like a fan. The down-flap of the wings moves the pigeon ahead; the feathers are tight together. On the up-flap, the feathers are spread, to let the air through.

The tail is used to steer and brake.

Pigeons have keen eyesight. But they can't see straight ahead from a distance. Pigeon eyes work separately—one eye looks to the left side, one to the right. In flight, this helps them see an enemy approaching.

Close up, they *can* see straight ahead. Sometimes, to look at something, they cock their head to one side.

They are certainly not fussy eaters. They eat stuff they find lying around—crumbs, a bit of cheese, a shred of meat from a sandwich. They don't have a keen sense of taste. (We have 9,000 taste buds in our mouth. A pigeon has only 37.)

This doesn't mean they'll eat any old thing. Sometimes you'll see a pigeon pick something up and drop it three or four times before eating it.

The pigeon is testing—trying to figure out whether the thing is okay to eat. They judge by the feel of it. And if they do happen to eat something that makes them sick—say, a certain kind of berry—they will never eat that same kind of thing again.

They eat a lot, very fast. They have a special pouch in

their throat, called the *crop*, where food is stored.

Sometimes you see pigeons pecking up sand and pebbles. They do this for a special reason. The pebbles go to a part of their stomach called the *gizzard*. Here, the pebbles roll around and help crush food.

Pigeons drink in an unusual way. They suck water up fast, like they're

using a straw. Other birds don't drink that way. Other birds take one sip at a time, each time lifting the head to swallow, then bending down for another sip.

The pigeon is the only bird that feeds its babies milk. Pigeon milk comes from the parent's crop. It's like milk with little cheeselike lumps in it. To get fed, the chick sticks its bill (and whole head, practically) into its parent's mouth. Both mother and father pigeons give pigeon milk.

People say, "There are so many pigeons. Why don't I ever see any baby pigeons?"

It's true. Most pigeons lay their eggs in hidden-away places. But sometimes they make a nest where you can see it. If you are lucky, you may have a chance to watch a mother and father pigeon bring up their babies.

17

Notes of
a pigeon-watcher

Two pigeons are hanging around a lot on a windowsill across the way. They coo, and nibble each other's necks.

Soon they get very busy. They fly back and forth, carrying twigs. They pile them up. They're making a nest. Are they going to have a family?

From now on, every time I look, there's always a pigeon sitting in that spot....

This is a good sign there may be eggs there. A mother pigeon lays two eggs, each weighing half an ounce. You hardly ever see pigeon eggs, because usually either the mother or father pigeon is sitting on them, to incubate them (keep them warm).

They take regular shifts. The mother sits from late afternoon through the night. In the morning, the father takes over and sits through the day.

After about 17 days, the eggs hatch. The babies peck their way out.

First week

I look out. It happened! There are two baby chicks. They're poking out from under the big pigeon. They're very small. They're covered with yellow fuzz.

As I watch, the big pigeon bends down and puts its beak right around a baby's mouth and head. The big one is feeding the baby pigeon milk. Then it feeds the second one.

When the feeding is over, the big one totally covers the babies with its body. If you looked out now, you wouldn't know the

19

babies were there. Now, all you can see is a big pigeon, sitting....

Second week

The chicks are bigger. They're losing their yellow fuzz. They're skinny and bald-looking now. Most of the time they sit close together, side by side. They have little round eyes. Do they see me looking at them?

They're alone now, a lot of the time. The mother and father keep coming back to feed them. But they stay only a short time. One parent is dusky black. The other is brown with a white head and tail. I wonder: Which is the mother, which is the father? Dusky-black is a bit bigger. Maybe he's the father.

The chicks are growing fast. They have some feathers now.

20

But under their wings, their skin is still bald-looking. They walk around now, in a sort of crouch. They lift their wings a bit. It's as though their wings feel heavy.

Now that they have feathers, I can tell them apart. One chick is solid brown. The other has a white head.

Third week

The chicks compete to get fed first. Each one tries to push the other away. White-head usually wins out. Sometimes there doesn't seem to be anything left for Brownie.

White-head stands facing inward doing fast practice wing-flaps. He can't fly yet. I guess he faces in so he doesn't take off by mistake. How does he know to face in?

Brownie just sits. She hasn't

21

done any wing-flaps yet. I worry. Is she getting enough to eat?

Here comes Dusky-black Pop, in for a feeding. Brownie stretches out her wings, keeping White-head back. For once, she has outmaneuvered him. This time, she's getting firsts on food. "Come on, Brownie," I whisper.

Feeding is pretty frantic. The chick's bill and part of its head are in Dusky-black Pop's mouth. The heads of parent and chick go up and down in a pumping motion. Their bodies quiver and shake. A bit of food dribbles down between their mouths.

Fourth week

Brownie's doing okay. She has tried a few wing-flaps. The chicks are now as tall as the parents. But not as plump.

Here comes White-head Mom.

22

The chicks bang at her with their wings. They peck her on the head. She scoots to the other end of the ledge. She gives a little burp. Then she turns back to feed them. Those pigeon parents are really something. She could have flown off when then were bopping and pecking at her. But she didn't....

Milk is made in the parents' crops for only about ten days. So the chicks are not getting pigeon milk anymore. Now they're being fed regurgitated food.

The chicks don't look so macho today. It's raining hard. They're huddled together. They look bedraggled and drippy.

Fifth week

This is it! Brownie's alone.

23

White-head has flown off. I hope he makes it on his own.

Brownie looks lonely. But she's not deserted. White-head Mom and Dusky-black Pop keep coming back to feed her. At night, the three roost together on the ledge.

Next day

I look out. Well, well. Brownie's gone, too. The ledge is empty. I've been watching them for more than a month. I guess I won't ever see them again. I hope they both lead good pigeon lives....

The day after that

Dusky-black Pop is sitting in the corner. White-head Mom is nibbling around his head. They both look tired. No wonder. They really worked hard, bringing up their babies.

24

From September to November pigeons *molt*. Old feathers fall out. New ones grow in. Soon the pigeons will start a new family.

Male pigeons are slightly larger than female; their neck feathers are a bit more shiny.

When a pigeon coos, often it's to keep in touch with its mate, who may be nearby but out of sight.

When pigeons are courting, a whole lot of cooing goes on. The male pigeon struts around the female. His crop is blown up, his feathers ruffled. The female sticks her beak into his. He feeds her regurgitated food. This is called "billing." It's a sign the pigeons are going to mate.

Pigeon pairs stay together for life. Often, they raise 5 or 6 or even more broods (families) a year.

A young pigeon is sometimes called a *squab*. If a pigeon stays healthy, it might live for 10 years or more.

Heroes, Helpers, Homers

Pigeons are very fast flyers. Some have been clocked at more than 90 miles per hour in races. (They can do this when there is a good tailwind to help them.) And they are especially good at finding their way home from hundreds, even thousands, of miles away.

In ancient days, when people learned about these special abilities that pigeons have, they put pigeons to work. In Greece, Rome, Egypt, and Persia, pigeons regularly carried news and messages from one city to another.

One emperor in India had 20,000 letter-carrying pigeons so he could

Egyptian carrier pigeons, about 45 B.C.

keep in touch with officials all over his empire.

In Greece, when the first Olympics were held in 776 B.C., how did people all over Greece find out who the winners were? Pigeons carried the news.

In 1815, how did the people of England first find out that their army had defeated Napoleon at the Battle of Waterloo? They got the news by carrier pigeon.

Banks in Paris and Brussels used to send stock market reports out by "Exchange Pigeons." In fact, until the telegraph (1836) and telephone (1875) were invented, the fastest way to send any kind of news was by pigeon.

Carrier pigeon, 1871.

Pigeons have even been honored as war heroes.

In World War I, a pigeon named Cher Ami ("dear friend" in French) saved the lives of many men of the "Lost Battalion," part of New York's 77th Division. During a battle in the Argonne Forest in France, they were cut off from the rest of the Allied troops and surrounded by the enemy. They were being fired on by their own artillery, who didn't know they were there.

They tried to get help. The first message they sent out was: "Many wounded. We cannot evacuate." But the pigeon carrying the message was shot down.

The second message was: "Men are suffering. Can support be sent…?" That pigeon didn't make it either.

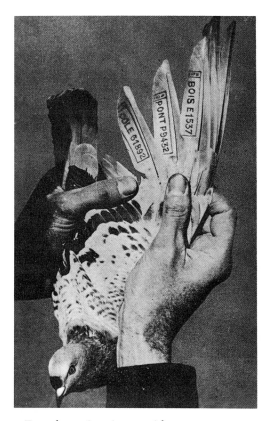

French carrier pigeon with war message on its feathers, 1914. (*Pont* means bridge; *Bois* means forest. The meaning of *Cole* is not known.)

They had one homing pigeon left—Cher Ami. The message was: "Our artillery is dropping a barrage on us. For heaven's sake, stop it!" Cher Ami was released. He was their last hope. As the men watched, they saw him shot down. But in a moment, he got up. As he flew over enemy fire, he had a leg shot off, and was shot in the breast. But he kept going. When he arrived, his feathers were covered with blood. But he got the message through, and saved lives.

At the end of the war, Cher Ami and more than 40 other pigeon heroes were sent back to the United States on the USS *Ohioan*. They were well cared for until they died. Cher Ami's body has been

Cher Ami

World War I homing pigeons. Sign on cage reads: "MILITARY HOMING PIGEONS. These are the birds that work to save the lives of our boys in France."

U.S. soldiers releasing carrier pigeons, 1943.

preserved and is now at the Smithsonian Institution in Washington, D.C.

In World War II, a British fishing boat was attacked by a German submarine. One of the crew members had a pet on board—a homing pigeon. As the boat was sinking, the wounded skipper attached a message to the pigeon: *"Nelson* attacked by subs. Send assistance." Skipper Crisp died on board. But the pigeon got the message through, and crew members were picked up. Skipper Crisp was posthumously awarded the Victoria Cross (the VC) for bravery. The pigeon was named after him, and called Crisp, VC.

In World War II, spies who parachuted behind enemy lines would

30

have a pigeon tied to their
chest. Later, the pigeon was
sent back with intelligence
information.

Advance foot patrols also
took pigeons with them.
When they learned about
enemy positions, they sent
word back by pigeon.

Army pigeons wore a
leather harness. The message
was in a tube attached to the
harness. When the pigeon
was flying, you couldn't see
its tube or harness. It looked
like just a wild bird. Sometimes the message was put in
a small container attached to
the pigeon's leg.

Right now, pigeons are
saving lives in peacetime, too.
They are trained in search-
and-rescue operations to find
ship and plane survivors in

Army carrier pigeon wearing a harness.

Aluminum message capsule

the sea. With their keen eyesight, pigeons are better able than people to spot the orange speck of a lifejacket.

The pigeons are kept in a special compartment in the search helicopter. When they see something, they peck at a keyboard. A light lights up. The copter pilot goes down. Pigeons can spot a survivor 90 percent of the time. People can do it only 40 percent of the time.

In a fishing village on a small island off the coast of France, there is a doctor, but no medical laboratory. When a blood test or some other test has to be done, the doctor sends the sample by pigeon to the mainland, where it is examined in a lab. The pigeon wears a vest. The vial with the sample is carried in a little vest pocket.

In May 1987, a pigeon helped a news photographer get a "scoop." While President and Nancy Reagan attended the memorial service for sailors who had died in the attack on the USS *Stark*, for security reasons no reporters were allowed to leave the naval station. But there was no rule against a pigeon leaving!

Photographer Robert Self brought a homing pigeon in with him—a 2-year-old, 14-ounce gray female who had won some 400-mile races. Self took his photos, attached the film to the pigeon's leg,

Robert Self removes pigeon from box to attach film capsule.

32

and set her free. An hour later, the pigeon returned home. This is how the *Jacksonville* (Florida) *Journal* got its photo before any other newspaper.

And so even now, in these days of jet planes, phones, and computers, sometimes the best way to send information is still by pigeon.

How do homing pigeons find their way home?

First, they circle around to get their bearings. Then they look at the sun. Scientists believe that pigeons can tell direction by the position of the sun in the sky.

When the sun is not visible, pigeons may be able to use the earth's magnetic field to help guide them. It's been discovered that pigeons have a bit of *magnetite* in their heads. This is the mineral from which the first

magnetic compasses were made. It is possible that this helps pigeons in their homing ability. In other words, each pigeon may carry its own compass right in its body. There is no proof of this as yet.

(It's interesting that salmon and monarch butterflies, who also do pinpoint navigation, have magnetite in their bodies, too.)

Many people raise homing pigeons, and race them as a hobby. The pigeons live in a *loft*, usually on the roof. This is the way they're trained: The owner first takes them one mile away, then two miles, then to more and more distant places before releasing them. Like any athlete, the pigeons improve with practice. Soon they are ready to race.

The pigeons are taken to a place miles from home. (There are 60-, 100-, and 400-mile races, or longer.) Each pigeon has a band with a number attached to its leg. They are released all at the same time.

Meanwhile, the owners have gone back home. When a pigeon returns, it enters the loft through a trapdoor. The owner takes the numbered leg band off and puts it into a special timing box that records the exact time of arrival.

Not all lofts are exactly the same distance from the start. So the winner is the pigeon that has reached home at the fastest average speed—not the one that gets back first.

From how far away can a homing pigeon find its way

back? This story will give us an idea.

A man in Long Island, New York, gave a "homer" to a friend who lived in Venezuela in South America. When the South American returned home, he let the New York pigeon out with the rest of his flock. This pigeon never came back with the others. The man thought it had been eaten by hawks, or had gotten lost. But the pigeon wasn't lost at all. It knew just where it was going! Three months later, it arrived back at its original home on Long Island. This was a flight of more than 2,000 miles.

Pigeons are in the family called *Columbidae* (from the Latin word *columba*, meaning dove). This family includes doves as well as pigeons. Usually, but not always, pigeons are larger than doves.

There are about 300 different species (types) of doves and pigeons. Not all live in cities. Some live in woods and fields. Fruit pigeons live in tropical forests.

They don't all look like city pigeons, either.

Tropical *fruit pigeons* are mostly green—good protective coloring for life in a tropical forest. Often they

Etching of the common pigeon from 1735.

36

have bright flecks of yellow or red. Some have many beautiful colors combined—yellow, orange, blue, green, and purple.

The *wood pigeon* is quite big—about 17 inches. It lives in the woods and eats buds, flowers, seeds, and leaves. It pecks up leaf bits at a rate of 100 per minute, often pecking up 35,000 bits in one day.

Tumbler pigeons do acrobatic loop-de-loops in the air.

The *pouter pigeon* puffs its neck out with air.

The *bleeding heart pigeon* of the Philippines has a red splotch on its breast that looks so much like blood that people who see it in a zoo often report an injured bird.

The *crowned pigeon* is the giant of pigeons. Some are as

Pouter pigeon

Bleeding heart pigeon

37

big as a turkey. It can measure 28 inches and weigh about 30 pounds. It lives in New Guinea and on Catalina Island, off the coast of California. It has a fanlike crest on its head.

Crowned pigeon

At one time, there were billions of beautiful gray-and-white *passenger pigeons*. Flocks were so large they blotted out the sun from view for days. John Audubon, the naturalist and artist, watched one flock that took three days to fly by. He estimated there were more than a billion birds in the flock.

Now there is not one passenger pigeon left in the world.

What happened?

They were too easy to kill.

Passenger pigeon

38

Landing, they were so thick in the trees, people could knock them off with a pole. People had "slaughtering parties." They killed passenger pigeons for fun. Billions were also killed to be sold as food for a penny apiece.

The last passenger pigeon was named Martha. She died in the Cincinnati Zoo in 1914.

Mass slaughter of passenger pigeons, 1867.

Have you ever heard the saying "dead as a dodo"? The dodo was a strange relative of the pigeon. It had a thick beak, stumpy wings, and an odd little curly-feathered tail. It was big; it weighed about 50 pounds. But it couldn't fly. It also was too easy to kill.

Dodoes used to live on islands off Africa. Like the passenger pigeon, it is now extinct.

Pigeons existed as long as two million years ago. We know this because fossils of pigeons have been found from those times. Now pigeons live in almost every part of the world except for Antarctica, the Arctic, and a few small islands.

Some pigeon words

pigeonhole: a small cubbyhole to put things in, usually on a desk (because pigeons squeeze into very small places)

stool pigeon: someone who betrays his friends (because people used to tie a pigeon to a stool as a decoy to attract other pigeons into a net to be trapped)

pigeon-toed: walking with your toes pointed inward

billing and cooing: two people acting very affectionate ("lovey-dovey") with each other (the way courting pigeons do)

Some people are fond of pigeons. They feed them seeds and crumbs. The pigeons get to know them. And even if the person is not throwing crumbs that day, the pigeons will still flock around.

Other people object to pigeons. Some farmers do, because pigeons eat grain. Some city people do, because of the mess caused by pigeon droppings. Pigeons can also carry disease. So watch them—but don't touch them, or pick them up.

City pigeons are survivors. Speedy, spunky, raising their families. Walking along in gangs, bobbing their heads as they walk. And making one of the nicest city sounds. Coo-roo…coo-roo…

A PIGEON ALBUM